HOW TO GIVE AWAY YOUR FAITH

IVP SIGNATURE BIBLE STUDIES

IVP SIGNATURE BIBLE STUDIES

BIBLE ✠ STUDY

PAUL E. LITTLE

WITH DALE LARSEN AND SANDY LARSEN

6 STUDIES FOR INDIVIDUALS OR GROUPS

An imprint of InterVarsity Press
Downers Grove, Illinois

InterVarsity Press, USA
P.O. Box 1400
Downers Grove, IL 60515-1426, USA
ivpress.com
email@ivpress.com

Inter-Varsity Press, England
36 Causton Street
London SW1P 4ST, England
ivpbooks.com
ivp@ivpbooks.com

This study guide is based on and adapts material from How to Give Away Your Faith *by Paul Little, second edition ©1988 by Marie Little.*

Originally published as Witnessing: How to Give Away Your Faith.

InterVarsity Press® is the book-publishing division of InterVarsity Christian Fellowship/USA®, a movement of students and faculty active on campus at hundreds of universities, colleges, and schools of nursing in the United States of America, and a member movement of the International Fellowship of Evangelical Students. For information about local and regional activities, visit intervarsity.org.

Inter-Varsity Press, England, is closely linked with the Universities and Colleges Christian Fellowship, a student movement connecting Christian Unions throughout Great Britain, and a member movement of the International Fellowship of Evangelical Students. Website: uccf.org.uk.

While any stories in this book are true, some names and identifying information may have been changed to protect the privacy of individuals.

Cover design and image composite: David Fassett
Interior design: Daniel van Loon
Images: light marble background : © Alexey Bykov / iStock / Getty Images Plus
*   rippled water: © Reimo Luck / EyeEm / Getty Images*
*   marble texture: © NK08gerd / iStock / Getty Images Plus*
*   glittering gold paint: © MirageC / Moment Collection / Getty Images*

ISBN 978-0-8308-4841-6 (print)
ISBN 978-0-8308-5794-4 (digital)

Printed in the United States of America ∞

InterVarsity Press is committed to ecological stewardship and to the conservation of natural resources in all our operations. This book was printed using sustainably sourced paper.

P 25 24 23 22 21 20 19 18 17 16 15 14 13 12 11 10 9 8 7 6 5 4 3 2 1

Y 38 37 36 35 34 33 32 31 30 29 28 27 26 25 24 23 22 21 20 19

CONTENTS

GETTING THE MOST OUT OF HOW TO GIVE AWAY YOUR FAITH BIBLE STUDY

KNOWING CHRIST is where faith begins. From there we are shaped through the essentials of discipleship: Bible study, prayer, Christian community, worship, and much more. We learn to grow in Christlike character, pursue justice, and share our faith with others. We persevere through doubts and gain wisdom for daily life. These are the topics woven into the IVP Signature Bible Studies. Working through this series will help you practice the essentials by exploring biblical truths found in classic books.

HOW IT'S PUT TOGETHER

Each session includes an opening quotation and suggested reading from the book *How to Give Away Your Faith*, a session goal to help guide your study, reflection questions to stir your thoughts on the topic, the text of the Bible passage, questions for exploring the passage, response questions to help you apply what you've learned, and a closing suggestion for prayer.

The workbook format is ideal for personal study and also allows group members to prepare in advance for discussions and to record discussion notes. The responses you write here can form a permanent record of your thoughts and spiritual progress.

Throughout the guide are study-note sidebars that may be useful for group leaders or individuals. These notes do not give the answers, but they do provide additional background information on certain questions and can challenge participants to think deeper or differently about the content.

WHAT KIND OF GUIDE IS THIS?

The studies are not designed to merely tell you what one person thinks. Instead, through inductive study they will help you discover for yourself what Scripture is saying. Each study deals with a particular passage—rather than jumping around the Bible—so that you can really delve into the biblical author's meaning in that context.

The studies ask three different kinds of questions about the Bible passage:

* *Observation* questions help you to understand the content of the passage by asking about the basic facts: who, what, when, where, and how.

* *Interpretation* questions delve into the meaning of the passage.

* *Application* questions help you discover implications for growing in Christ in your own life.

These three keys unlock the treasures of the biblical writings and help you live them out.

This is a thought-provoking guide. Each question assumes a variety of answers. Many questions do not have "right" answers, particularly questions that aim at meaning or application. Instead, the questions should inspire readers to explore the passage more thoroughly.

This study guide is flexible. You can use it for individual study, but it is also great for a variety of groups—student, professional, neighborhood, or church groups. Each study takes about forty-five minutes in a group setting or thirty minutes in personal study.

SUGGESTIONS FOR INDIVIDUAL STUDY

1. This guide is based on a classic book that will enrich your spiritual life. If you have not read *How to Give Away Your Faith*, you may want to read the portion recommended in the "Read" section before you begin your study. The ideas in the book will enhance your study, but the Bible text will be the focus of each session.

2. Begin each session with prayer, asking God to speak to you from his Word about this particular topic.

3. As you read the Scripture passage, reproduced for you from the New International Version, you may wish to mark phrases that seem important. Note in the margin any questions that come to your mind.

4. Close with the suggestion for prayer. Speak to God about insights you have gained. Tell him of any desires you have for specific growth. Ask him to help you as you attempt to live out the principles described in that passage. You may wish to write your own prayer in this guide or in a journal.

SUGGESTIONS FOR GROUP MEMBERS

Joining a Bible study group can be a great avenue to spiritual growth. Here are a few guidelines that will help you as you participate in the studies in this guide.

1. Reading the recommended portion of *How to Give Away Your Faith* before or after each session will enhance your study and understanding of the themes in this guide.

2. These studies use methods of inductive Bible study, which focuses on a particular passage of Scripture and works on it

in depth. So try to dive into the given text instead of referring to other Scripture passages.

3. Questions are designed to help a group discuss together a passage of Scripture in order to understand its content, meaning, and implications. Most people are either natural talkers or natural listeners, yet this type of study works best if all members participate more or less evenly. Try to curb any natural tendency to either excessive talking or excessive quiet. You and the rest of the group will benefit!

4. Most questions in this guide allow for a variety of answers. If you disagree with someone else's comment, gently say so. Then explain your own point of view from the passage before you.

5. Be willing to lead a discussion, if asked. Much of the preparation for leading has already been accomplished in the writing of this guide.

6. Respect the privacy of people in your group. Many people share things within the context of a Bible study group that they do not want to be public knowledge. Assume that personal information spoken within the group setting is private, unless you are specifically told otherwise.

7. We recommend that all groups agree on a few basic guidelines. You may wish to adapt this list to your situation:

   a. Anything said in this group is considered confidential and will not be discussed outside the group unless specific permission is given to do so.

   b. We will provide time for each person present to talk if he or she feels comfortable doing so.

   c. We will talk about ourselves and our own situations, avoiding conversation about other people.

d. We will listen attentively to each other.

e. We will pray for each other.

8. Enjoy your study. Prepare to grow!

SUGGESTIONS FOR GROUP LEADERS

There are specific suggestions to help you in the "Leading a Small Group" section. It describes how to lead a group discussion, gives helpful tips on group dynamics, and suggests ways to deal with problems that may arise during the discussion. With such helps, someone with little or no experience can lead an effective group study. Read this section carefully, even if you are leading only one group meeting.

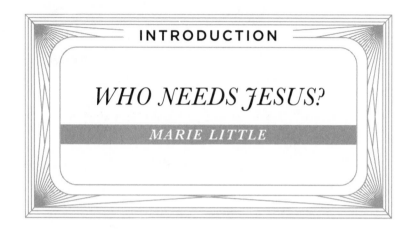

INTRODUCTION

WHO NEEDS JESUS?

MARIE LITTLE

So you want to witness for Jesus Christ! I did too, but I didn't have a clue how to do it without stubbing my toe in the process.

How about you? Do you know how to connect people with the good news, and connect the good news with people? Do you know how to communicate with people to whom the gospel seems alien? How do you talk about Jesus Christ with

* the factory worker whose job has just been outsourced overseas?

* the "whatever" partying twenty-something (or thirty-something) across the hall?

* the victim of unwanted divorce or abuse who can no longer trust anyone?

* the university religion major who mocks your defense of biblical teachings with, "Come on, this is the twenty-first century!"

* the hard-working manager of the local convenience store?

* that young woman you know who's gotten everything she's ever wanted?

* the high school student who's about to drop out of school because of drug abuse?

* the stay-at-home mom struggling to keep up with small children, her peers, and multiple community demands?

* the successful businessperson who is chronically exhausted?

* those nearest to you: your family, your friends, your next-door neighbors?

It's easy to say, "God so loved the world . . ." but what do those words mean for the people you know? What can you say to them about God that will make sense in their everyday lives?

TWO ESSENTIAL INGREDIENTS FOR FAITH

To know Jesus Christ personally involves two things. The first is a commitment, a time when we make a conscious decision: "Yes, I do want to belong to you, Lord Jesus Christ." That commitment extends to a continual, lifetime involvement of one's self with the living Lord. A genuine relationship means more than merely knowing the facts about another person; it involves knowing the entire person. Similarly, a relationship with Jesus Christ begins with making contact with him personally by praying to him and inviting him into our lives to be our living Lord and Savior. For all of us, this is the first step.

The second thing is love and obedience to our living Lord and Savior. It is unthinkable to consider a relationship with the Lord Jesus that is less than one hundred percent. He is the spectacular Lord from heaven; he is the Lord of all the earth. When we let this fact get fully into the marrow of our bones, we know that willing obedience to him is an immense privilege.

Once we understand these basics, we can become effective ambassadors of Christ—the greatest challenge and the highest honor that will ever be given to us.

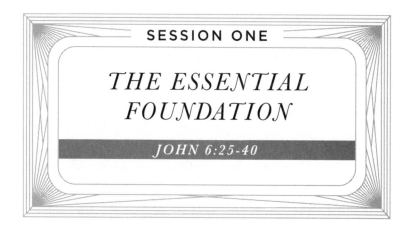

THE ESSENTIAL FOUNDATION

JOHN 6:25-40

I WILL NEVER FORGET an Asian Christian, a judge, who chatted with me in the dining commons of Harvard University. He said, "I wish you Christians in the West could realize that we from the East, who have gone through the ravages of war, starvation, suffering, political turmoil, and the loss of loved ones, have a profound wound in our hearts." He continued, "I know that essentially the gospel is God's message of love and that while it has social implications, it is directed primarily to the spiritual need for redemption. But it would mean so much if only we saw that you understood this wound in our hearts."

Many of those we rub shoulders with carry just such a "profound wound" in their hearts. Their response to us and the good news we share depends a lot on whether they think we really understand and care. A Native American proverb states, "One should say nothing to another until he has walked in his moccasins." In spirit, at least, we need to walk where others walk. When we can reflect back to them their thoughts and feelings in our own words, they will begin to trust us. From there they will be willing to think seriously about the things we care about.

The people who God has used throughout the centuries are those who have both known their Bible well and known others well. Loving both, they have made the Word relevant to others. So we begin with the biblical foundation for witnessing.

SESSION GOAL	READ
Realize that all people have a deep spiritual hunger that only Christ can satisfy.	Chapter one of *How to Give Away Your Faith*

 REFLECT

✳ Think of some of the people you know, and name some of their needs—relational, spiritual, physical.

✳ Which of those needs have you also experienced?

 STUDY

On the far side of the Sea of Galilee, Jesus met the needs of a huge crowd of people by miraculously feeding them (see John 6:1-13). During the night he and his disciples crossed the lake to Capernaum. His absence caused a stir the next day, and the crowd went searching for him. ***Read John 6:25-40.***

25When they found him on the other side of the lake, they asked him, "Rabbi, when did you get here?"

26Jesus answered, "Very truly I tell you, you are looking for me, not because you saw the signs I performed but because you ate the loaves and had your fill. [27]Do not work for food that spoils, but for food that endures to eternal life, which the Son of Man will give you. For on him God the Father has placed his seal of approval."

[28]Then they asked him, "What must we do to do the works God requires?"

[29]Jesus answered, "The work of God is this: to believe in the one he has sent."

[30]So they asked him, "What sign then will you give that we may see it and believe you? What will you do? [31]Our ancestors ate the manna in the wilderness; as it is written: 'He gave them bread from heaven to eat.'"

[32]Jesus said to them, "Very truly I tell you, it is not Moses who has given you the bread from heaven, but it is my Father who gives you the true bread from heaven. [33]For the bread of God is the bread that comes down from heaven and gives life to the world."

[34]"Sir," they said, "always give us this bread."

[35]Then Jesus declared, "I am the bread of life. Whoever comes to me will never go hungry, and whoever believes in me will never be thirsty. [36]But as I told you, you have seen me and still you do not believe. [37]All those the Father gives me will come to me, and whoever comes to me I will never drive away. [38]For I have come down from heaven not to do my will but to do the will of him who sent me. [39]And this is the will of him who sent me, that I shall lose none of all those he has given me, but raise them up at the last day. [40]For my Father's will is that everyone who looks to the Son and believes in him shall have eternal life, and I will raise them up at the last day."

1. What everyday symbol runs throughout Jesus' words in this passage?

2. How did Jesus use the miracle of the preceding day to point the people to their greater spiritual need (vv. 26-27)?

3. The people's first response was "What must we do to do the works God requires?" (v. 28). How do people today try to earn God's approval through performance?

4. How does a "works" mentality differ from what Jesus called the work of God (v. 29)?

Consider the things we *do* as well as the things we *don't do* in order to be regarded as "good." Although any of those actions can be motivated by a pure heart, they are sometimes done simply to earn God's favor.

5. The people's second response was to change the subject from what God requires to what they required of Jesus (vv. 30-31). They demanded the evidence of a miraculous sign so they could believe. What excuses have you heard people give for not believing in Jesus? (Think especially of statements like "I could believe if . . .")

Every Jew would have known about the miracle of God providing manna for the Israelites: "bread from heaven" (see Exodus 16). The people who heard Jesus were initially astonished by the miraculous multiplication of bread and fish, but their response was to require more of Jesus—more signs and miracles—in order to believe.

6. How did Jesus maintain their interest while steering the conversation away from physical food to spiritual food (vv. 32-33)?

7. How did Jesus promise to fulfill the spiritual yearnings of those who come to him (vv. 35-40)?

8. How has Jesus fulfilled your spiritual yearning?

> "Comes" and "believes" in the original Greek (v. 35)
> indicate a continual coming and believing. This
> Scripture says that all those who *keep on coming*
> *and believing* will not hunger and thirst.

RESPOND

✳ Of the people (especially non-Christians) you have regular
contact with, who would you like to spend extra time with
this week? Listen attentively to this person to gain understanding of his or her wounds, needs, and hurts. Identify
some ways you can offer encouragement, perhaps helping
with his or her everyday needs.

✳ How might you lead a conversation beyond everyday things
toward an awareness that God can help?

PRAY

Talk to God about any fears you have about witnessing to the person
you are thinking of. Also pray for that person to look beyond the
physical level of life and to turn to the Lord with every need, in-
cluding the need for salvation.

THE EFFECTIVE AMBASSADOR

2 CORINTHIANS 5:11-21

ABOUT ONCE EVERY SIX MONTHS the pressure to witness would reach explosive levels inside me. Not knowing any better, I would suddenly lunge at someone and spout Scripture verses with a sort of glazed look in my eye. But I honestly didn't expect any response. As soon as my victim indicated a lack of interest, I'd begin to edge away with a sigh of relief and breathe the consoling thought, "Everyone who wants to live a godly life in Christ Jesus will be persecuted" (2 Timothy 3:12). Duty done, I'd draw back into my martyr's shell for another six months of hibernation until the internal pressure again became intolerable and drove me out. It really shocked me when I finally realized that I, not the cross, was offending people. My inept, unwittingly rude, even stupid approach to them was responsible for their rejection of me and the gospel message.

Does witnessing mean spouting a slew of Bible verses at non-Christians? Not quite. Witnessing goes far beyond what we say at certain inspired moments. It involves all that we are and do. It's a way of life—the "art" of explaining to someone who Jesus is, and why trusting him as Lord and Savior is the best news in the world.

Witnessing is that deep-seated conviction that the greatest thing I can do for others is to introduce them to Jesus Christ. We are "Christ's ambassadors" (2 Corinthians 5:20). In our role as witnesses, we are God's representatives, appointed to be his messengers. God actually makes his appeal to the world through us Christians (2 Corinthians 5:18-21). Consider the tremendous appointment of being an ambassador for the foreign policy of the kingdom of heaven!

SESSION GOAL	READ
Determine to be better and more faithful ambassadors for Christ.	Chapter two of *How to Give Away Your Faith*

 **REFLECT**

✳ What are some of your greatest fears about witnessing for Christ?

✳ Think of a time when you had a clear opportunity to witness to someone . . . and *didn't*. How did you feel afterward? What did you say to yourself? What did you say to the Lord?

 **STUDY**

READ 2 CORINTHIANS 5:11-21.

[11]Since, then, we know what it is to fear the Lord, we try to persuade others. What we are is plain to God, and I

hope it is also plain to your conscience. [12]We are not trying to commend ourselves to you again, but are giving you an opportunity to take pride in us, so that you can answer those who take pride in what is seen rather than in what is in the heart. [13]If we are "out of our mind," as some say, it is for God; if we are in our right mind, it is for you. [14]For Christ's love compels us, because we are convinced that one died for all, and therefore all died. [15]And he died for all, that those who live should no longer live for themselves but for him who died for them and was raised again.

[16]So from now on we regard no one from a worldly point of view. Though we once regarded Christ in this way, we do so no longer. [17]Therefore, if anyone is in Christ, the new creation has come: The old has gone, the new is here! [18]All this is from God, who reconciled us to himself through Christ and gave us the ministry of reconciliation: [19]that God was reconciling the world to himself in Christ, not counting people's sins against them. And he has committed to us the message of reconciliation. [20]We are therefore Christ's ambassadors, as though God were making his appeal through us. We implore you on Christ's behalf: Be reconciled to God. [21]God made him who had no sin to be sin for us, so that in him we might become the righteousness of God.

1. What does this passage urge readers to do and become?

2. Paul explained the motivating force behind his ministry of preaching the gospel. What was it? (Notice especially verses 11, 14-15.)

> It is interesting that Paul appealed to both "fear" and "love" to explain his motive for witness. Keep in mind that to "fear the Lord" (v. 11) means "reverential fear ... of God, as a controlling motive of the life, in matters spiritual and moral, not a mere fear of His power and righteous retribution, but a wholesome dread of displeasing Him."*

3. What do you think it means to stop regarding people from a worldly point of view (v. 16)?

4. What evidences could you give that you are a "new creation" in Christ (v. 17)?

> Identifying how Christ has changed us gives substance to our witness. Rather than a vague "Christ made me a new person," we help people understand what Christ means in our lives by describing specific changes: "Christ has changed my heart toward ..." or "Christ has eased my anxiety about ..."

5. What work begun by Christ are we privileged to carry on (vv. 18-19)?

6. Consider the designation "Christ's ambassadors" (v. 20). What light does that phrase shed on how we should live among nonbelievers?

7. In what sense does the ruler (God) make his appeal through his ambassadors (us) (v. 20)?

Consider the role and responsibility of a nation's ambassador. Ambassadors do not make unilateral decisions regarding governance and treaties—they accurately represent their government and nation. Ambassadors are the messengers who appeal to foreign nations on behalf of their home country.

8. Perhaps you don't feel worthy of being Christ's ambassador. What do you find in this passage to reassure you that God has qualified you for this position?

 **RESPOND**

✳ Briefly review your past week. In what areas do you view yourself as Christ's ambassador? Plan some specific ways you can better represent Christ to your world this coming week. Consider actions, words, and attitudes.

✳ If you are meeting with a group, follow up on how each of you did with your commitment to spend time with a particular person last week. How will you continue to follow up with that person?

 **PRAY**

Thank God for the difference Christ has made in your life. Thank him for the great privilege of serving as his ambassador. Pray for the needs of the person you chose to spend time with last week.

---

*W. E. Vine, *An Expository Dictionary of New Testament Words,* vol. 2 (London: Oliphants, 1940), 84.

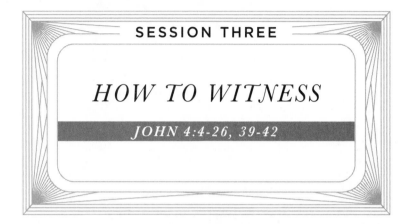

HOW TO WITNESS

JOHN 4:4-26, 39-42

FOR HIS DAY, Jesus did a most remarkable thing when he was in Samaria. In John 4:39-41, he talked with a number of Samaritans from Sychar who knew the woman at the well, and at their urging, stayed with them for two days. He gladly met the woman's friends and acquaintances. Besides that, he must have slept in their beds, eaten their food, and talked to them far into the night. This kind of interaction between Jews and Samaritans was unthinkable, yet Jesus always broke barriers; he refused to consider what mere tradition demanded. These people mattered to him. They were not simply statistics. And as verse 41 puts it, "Because of his words many more became believers."

To contact others socially we may need to go out of our usual path, altering our own plans as Jesus did with the Samaritans. Breaking down barriers may require such radical efforts. But what better way to express the love of Jesus Christ and demonstrate how much we value others?

SESSION GOAL	READ
Analyze the witnessing model of Jesus' encounter with the woman at the well in Samaria.	Chapter three of *How to Give Away Your Faith*

⚬ REFLECT ⚬

✳ Complete this statement: "I find it easy to turn a conversation toward spiritual issues when the other person
_____."

✳ And complete this statement: "There are certain people who
I don't think would ever be open to talk about Christ
because _____."

⚬ STUDY ⚬

READ JOHN 4:4-26, 39-42.

⁴Now he had to go through Samaria. ⁵So he came to a
town in Samaria called Sychar, near the plot of ground
Jacob had given to his son Joseph. ⁶Jacob's well was there,
and Jesus, tired as he was from the journey, sat down by the
well. It was about noon.

⁷When a Samaritan woman came to draw water, Jesus
said to her, "Will you give me a drink?" ⁸(His disciples had
gone into the town to buy food.)

⁹The Samaritan woman said to him, "You are a Jew and
I am a Samaritan woman. How can you ask me for a drink?"
(For Jews do not associate with Samaritans.)

¹⁰Jesus answered her, "If you knew the gift of God and
who it is that asks you for a drink, you would have asked
him and he would have given you living water."

¹¹"Sir," the woman said, "you have nothing to draw with and the well is deep. Where can you get this living water? ¹²Are you greater than our father Jacob, who gave us the well and drank from it himself, as did also his sons and his livestock?"

¹³Jesus answered, "Everyone who drinks this water will be thirsty again, ¹⁴but whoever drinks the water I give them will never thirst. Indeed, the water I give them will become in them a spring of water welling up to eternal life."

¹⁵The woman said to him, "Sir, give me this water so that I won't get thirsty and have to keep coming here to draw water."

¹⁶He told her, "Go, call your husband and come back."

¹⁷"I have no husband," she replied.

Jesus said to her, "You are right when you say you have no husband. ¹⁸The fact is, you have had five husbands, and the man you now have is not your husband. What you have just said is quite true."

¹⁹"Sir," the woman said, "I can see that you are a prophet. ²⁰Our ancestors worshiped on this mountain, but you Jews claim that the place where we must worship is in Jerusalem."

²¹"Woman," Jesus replied, "believe me, a time is coming when you will worship the Father neither on this mountain nor in Jerusalem. ²²You Samaritans worship what you do not know; we worship what we do know, for salvation is from the Jews. ²³Yet a time is coming and has now come when the true worshipers will worship the Father in the Spirit and in truth, for they are the kind of worshipers the Father seeks. ²⁴God is spirit, and his worshipers must worship in the Spirit and in truth."

²⁵The woman said, "I know that Messiah" (called Christ)

"is coming. When he comes, he will explain everything to us."
²⁶Then Jesus declared, "I, the one speaking to you—
I am he."...

³⁹Many of the Samaritans from that town believed in
him because of the woman's testimony, "He told me everything I ever did." ⁴⁰So when the Samaritans came to him,
they urged him to stay with them, and he stayed two days.
⁴¹And because of his words many more became believers.

⁴²They said to the woman, "We no longer believe just
because of what you said; now we have heard for ourselves,
and we know that this man really is the Savior of the world."

1. The Samaritan woman was drawn into a very unlikely discussion with a stranger. What are some elements of the conversation that kept her attention?

2. In Jesus' time, Jews normally avoided travel through Samaria by
   crossing the Jordan River and going the long way around. What
   is implied in the phrase "he had to go through Samaria" (v. 4)?

3. In what circumstances are you tempted to avoid nonbelievers?

When Samaria fell to the Assyrians in 722 BC, the Israelites were taken into exile and their land was repopulated with foreigners. The newcomers began to worship the Lord along with their own gods (2 Kings 17:5-6, 24-33). Because the Samaritans were not true Israelites in either lineage or religion, they were despised by the Jews.

4. Notice how Jesus opened the conversation with the Samaritan woman (v. 7). How did he begin talking with her?

5. By what steps did Jesus lead the conversation beyond water to the woman's deeper spiritual needs?

The fact that Jesus spoke to this woman at all was highly unusual. As a man, he spoke to her—a woman. As a rabbi, he spoke to her—an immoral woman. As a Jew, he spoke to her—a Samaritan. So Jesus' simple request for water likely surprised the woman.

6. The turning point in this conversation came when the woman expressed an interest in getting the "living water" (v. 15). How did Jesus use his knowledge of her living situation to point out her spiritual need?

Previously, when Jesus offered "the true bread from heaven," his hearers immediately demanded, "Sir, always give us this bread" (John 6:34). When Jesus offered living water to the woman at the well, she said, "Sir, give me this water." In both cases Jesus made people curious enough to listen eagerly to what he said next.

7. How did the woman try to avoid the implications of her lifestyle, and how did Jesus bring her back to the real issue (vv. 16-24)?

8. What were the wider results of this conversation by Jacob's well (vv. 39-42)?

When we influence someone for Christ, it rarely ends there. People live in many intersecting circles of family, coworkers, and friends. Our witness spreads out through these people. Some we may meet; others we may never know about.

⚒ RESPOND ⚒

✳ What would it mean for you to go out of your usual way to contact a person who needs Christ? What would make the extra effort worthwhile?

✳ Here are some ideas of things to say to turn a conversation to spiritual things. Which of these might feel comfortable to you?

- ☐ I've found that God can help when things get tough.
- ☐ I know God cares for you. That's why Jesus came to this earth.
- ☐ Would you like me to pray for you this week?
- ☐ I can see that you've done as well as you can, but only God's love can help you cope with this situation.
- ☐ I've faced similar pressures, and I know decisions are not easy to make. Here's how God has helped me . . .
- ☐ Jesus has comforted me in hard times.

✳ Plan now to alter your usual routine to talk with someone who needs to hear about the Lord. Also be alert to unexpected people who God might put in your path.

⚒ PRAY ⚒

Pray for openness to opportunities to witness to people outside your normal social circle.

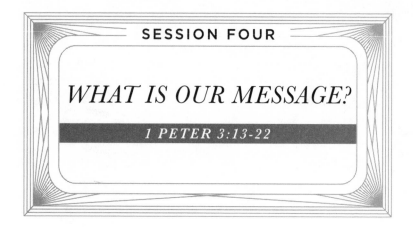

WHAT IS OUR MESSAGE?

1 PETER 3:13-22

A CHRISTIAN STUDENT was driving with a non-Christian along the highway in Pennsylvania. They passed a sign that said, "Jesus saves." The companion remarked very sincerely, "That's something I never thought of before. If Jesus is thrifty, I ought to be too!"

When we communicate the gospel, it is essential to realize that Christianity is not about a philosophy or a way of life, but about a living person: Jesus Christ. Unless non-Christians see that the issue is their own relationship to this person, we have failed.

Confusion about the true, ungarbled definition of Christianity is a virtual epidemic. The issue is not what church people should belong to, or what amusements they should or should not attend. Here are some of the popular misconceptions of what Christianity is.

Christianity is not . . .

* regularly attending church.

* keeping up a family heritage.

* belonging to a certain culture.

* following the teachings of Christ.

⁕ avoiding certain negative behaviors.

⁕ doing charitable works.

⁕ believing the facts about Jesus Christ.

Christianity is about Jesus Christ himself—who he is, what he has done, and how he can be known in personal experience.

SESSION GOAL	READ
Focus on the person of Jesus Christ as the center of our witness.	Chapters four and five of *How to Give Away Your Faith*

REFLECT

⁕ What are some misconceptions you have had about Christianity? (Don't be afraid to include those you've had even after becoming a Christian!)

⁕ How are you tempted to get distracted from the truth that "Christianity is about Jesus Christ himself"?

STUDY

Peter wrote to believers who were scattered because of persecution. He knew a lot about persecution, having been imprisoned and beaten several times for his preaching. ***Read 1 Peter 3:13-22.***

¹³Who is going to harm you if you are eager to do good? ¹⁴But even if you should suffer for what is right, you are blessed. "Do not fear their threats; do not be frightened." ¹⁵But in your hearts revere Christ as Lord. Always be prepared to give an answer to everyone who asks you to give the reason for the hope that you have. But do this with gentleness and respect, ¹⁶keeping a clear conscience, so that those who speak maliciously against your good behavior in Christ may be ashamed of their slander. ¹⁷For it is better, if it is God's will, to suffer for doing good than for doing evil. ¹⁸For Christ also suffered once for sins, the righteous for the unrighteous, to bring you to God. He was put to death in the body but made alive in the Spirit. ¹⁹After being made alive, he went and made proclamation to the imprisoned spirits— ²⁰to those who were disobedient long ago when God waited patiently in the days of Noah while the ark was being built. In it only a few people, eight in all, were saved through water, ²¹and this water symbolizes baptism that now saves you also—not the removal of dirt from the body but the pledge of a clear conscience toward God. It saves you by the resurrection of Jesus Christ, ²²who has gone into heaven and is at God's right hand—with angels, authorities and powers in submission to him.

1. In times of persecution, what did Peter say is vital for believers to focus on, and why?

2. Think of times you face opposition to your witness for Christ. What difference does it make in your behavior if in your heart you continue to revere Christ as Lord (v. 15)?

> In times of opposition, many other thoughts threaten to crowd out thoughts of Jesus: thoughts of how unjust the attack is, plans for revenge, feelings of self-pity or self-righteousness, etc.

3. What are some ways that we can show "gentleness and respect" as we answer people who oppose us (v. 15)?

4. When we're challenged by people, it's important to be able to give "the reason for the hope that you have" (v. 15). What do verses 18-22 demonstrate about the reason for our hope?

> Jesus suffered for us—took the sentence of death that belongs to us because we have all broken God's moral law. He stepped into our place to receive our judgment, so we could be forgiven. The result is to restore us to the relationship that God intended for us at creation. You might want to list these key facts about Jesus on a notecard to keep for reference when witnessing.

5. How has the gospel given you hope?

6. Why is keeping a clear conscience so important (vv. 16-17)?

> We know too many examples of people who try to convince others to follow Jesus, yet their own lives don't reflect his character. We will never be morally perfect in this world, but we can be transparent before God.

7. What central, nonnegotiable facts about Jesus are emphasized in verse 18?

RESPOND

❋ As you witness to certain people, what peripheral issues do you tend to get bogged down in? How can you get back to the central facts about Jesus?

❋ When do you especially need to keep in your mind and heart that Christ is Lord?

PRAY

Worship the Lord who died for your sins to bring you to God and who rose again. Pray for your friends who need to know him.

BELIEVE, RECEIVE, BECOME

The truths about Jesus Christ are more than theological facts. They require more than a nod of the head in agreement. They demand a response that involves a change of mind about how we view sin and a determination to turn to God.

The mind must comprehend the holiness of God and our own utter failure and inability to measure up to God's standards of perfection. Paul, in his defense before Agrippa, said he preached that both Jews and Gentiles "should repent and turn to God" (Acts 26:20). The substance of repentance is the repudiation of our self-centered lives and making Christ and his will the center of our lives.

The emotions are also involved in turning to God. In contrast to being superficially sorry for sin, "godly sorrow brings repentance that leads to salvation and leaves no regret" (2 Corinthians 7:10). Although feelings are not a sufficient gauge of genuine repentance, we should expect to experience some feeling about turning away from ourselves and turning to God.

The final test of true repentance involves the will. The prodigal son not only came to his senses intellectually, but he acted: "'I will set out and go back to my father.' ... So he got up and went to his father" (Luke 15:18,20).

At this point, people need to take that first step of coming to trust Jesus Christ personally. But it is not always easy for us to vividly explain this experience. Vague abstract terms like believe and have faith do not concretely describe what is involved in becoming a Christian.

It seems to me that the clearest statement in the New

Testament on how to become a Christian is John 1:12: "Yet to all who did receive him, to those who believed in his name, he gave the right to become children of God." There are three operative verbs in this statement: *believe*, *receive*, *become*. Someone has said that in becoming a Christian there is something to be believed and someone to be received. This aptly sums up John 1:12.

It is significant that marriage is one of the illustrations the New Testament uses for becoming and being a Christian. Merely believing in a man or a woman, however intense that feeling might be, does not make one married. Even if we are emotionally involved, we still are not married. For example, for a man to become married, he first believes in a woman and then must receive her into his life. In order to get married, he finally has to come to a commitment of the will and say "I do," committing himself to the other person and thereby establishing a relationship. It involves total commitment of intellect, emotions, and will.

Mere intellectual assent to facts about Jesus does not make a person a Christian, any more than mere intellectual assent to facts about marriage makes a person married. Being a Christian requires committing ourselves to a living Lord. This commitment depends on a relationship of love and obedience. We must believe in Jesus, personally receive him into our lives, and thus become children of God.

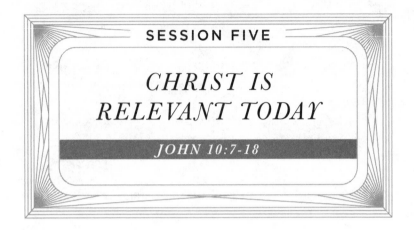

THE QUESTION UPPERMOST in people's minds today is not, "Is Christianity true?" but "Is it relevant?" Their response to our witness may be, "So I believe what you've said about Jesus Christ—so what? What's it got to do with contemporary life? What's it got to do with me?"

If we want to speak of Jesus Christ today, we need to have in the forefront of our minds how he is personally relevant to us. From there we can consider how to relate the events that took place two thousand years ago to life today.

We can help people see the significance of faith by following Jesus' model. John 10 shows us how deeply Christ, the Good Shepherd, involves himself in the lives of his followers.

SESSION GOAL	READ
Understand how Christ speaks to the needs people feel.	Chapters six and seven of *How to Give Away Your Faith*

REFLECT

✳ What are some areas of your life where it is easy to think of Christ being involved?

✳ What are the areas of your life that you have trouble thinking of Christ being involved?

STUDY

Jesus' ministry was approaching a crisis. The more he said and did, the more he angered the powerful people. The issue came down to who would trust him enough to listen and follow him. *Read John 10:7-18.*

> [7] Therefore Jesus said again, "Very truly I tell you, I am the gate for the sheep. [8] All who have come before me are thieves and robbers, but the sheep have not listened to them. [9] I am the gate; whoever enters through me will be saved. They will come in and go out, and find pasture. [10] The thief comes only to steal and kill and destroy; I have come that they may have life, and have it to the full.
>
> [11] "I am the good shepherd. The good shepherd lays down his life for the sheep. [12] The hired hand is not the shepherd and does not own the sheep. So when he sees the wolf coming, he abandons the sheep and runs away. Then the wolf attacks the flock and scatters it. [13] The man runs away because he is a hired hand and cares nothing for the sheep.

¹⁴"I am the good shepherd; I know my sheep and my sheep know me— ¹⁵just as the Father knows me and I know the Father—and I lay down my life for the sheep. ¹⁶I have other sheep that are not of this sheep pen. I must bring them also. They too will listen to my voice, and there shall be one flock and one shepherd. ¹⁷The reason my Father loves me is that I lay down my life—only to take it up again. ¹⁸No one takes it from me, but I lay it down of my own accord. I have authority to lay it down and authority to take it up again. This command I received from my Father."

1. How did Jesus use an extended word picture to explain his trustworthy character?

To express his all-sufficiency?

Even though the ins and outs of shepherding are foreign to many of us, in the Near Eastern cultural setting, sheep and shepherding were easily understood as symbols of the relationship between God and humanity. For examples from the Old Testament, see Psalm 23; Isaiah 53:6; Jeremiah 23:1, 50:6; and Ezekiel 34:6, 11-16.

2. What is the contrast between the hired hand's involvement and the sheep and the good shepherd's involvement (vv. 11-13)?

Shepherds who worked as hired hands were not under any obligation should the sheep come under attack by wild animals. But here, Jesus is making an indictment against religious leaders who act as though they are hired hands—under no obligation to protect the people they lead—because they don't care for people the way Jesus cares for people. What matters to God should matter to us.

3. Who or what are some of the "hired hands," or false sources of security, that people rely on today?

4. How does the Good Shepherd show the depth of his commitment to the sheep (vv. 14-18)?

Jesus says that his sheep listen to his voice (John 10:16, 27). The world is full of noise—competing messages that can drown out the voice of the Good Shepherd. In order to *follow* Jesus more closely, we'll need to train ourselves to *listen* more carefully and recognize his voice.

5. How does the picture of Christ as shepherd speak to your needs . . .

for purpose?

for peace?

for relationship?

for freedom from the fear of death?

6. How have you experienced life "to the full" (v. 10) in Christ?

⚜ RESPOND ⚜

✳ Think of people you know who have entrusted their lives to the "hired hands" and been abandoned. This week, how can you communicate to someone how Christ the Good Shepherd has kept his commitment to you?

✳ Consider the people you are praying for, that they will come to know Christ. How will you stay faithful to them in the face of setbacks or disappointments along the way?

⚜ PRAY ⚜

Thank the Lord for his faithfulness. Ask him to keep your heart open to opportunities to introduce people to him.

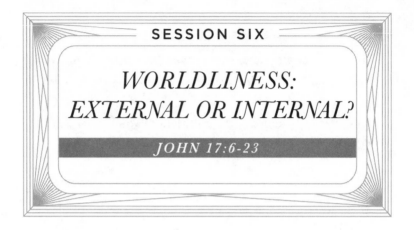

WORLDLINESS: EXTERNAL OR INTERNAL?

JOHN 17:6-23

GENUINE CHRISTIANS WANT TO live holy lives. But Satan tries to convince us that if we clan together and avoid all unnecessary contact with non-Christians, we will not be contaminated by the world around us. By his devilish logic he has persuaded us that true spirituality means separating ourselves from the world around us. Some Christians have told me with evident pride that no non-Christian has ever been inside their homes. With an air of "spirituality," they have boasted that they have no non-Christian friends. No wonder they have never had the joy of introducing someone to the Savior!

When we examine the teaching of the New Testament, we discover that separation from the world does involve pulling back from and avoiding evil. But in the overall view of the New Testament, this cannot mean isolation from the world! In his prayer for us in John 17, Jesus made this clear. In fact withdrawal from those who do not know Jesus Christ is outright disobedience to the will of the Lord.

SESSION GOAL	READ
Examine Christ's concerns for us and his desire for how we ought to live in the world.	Chapters eight through ten of *How to Give Away Your Faith*

REFLECT

✳ I would define *worldliness* as:

✳ One way *not* to be worldly is:

STUDY

Facing his imminent arrest and execution, Jesus was still mindful of his disciples—and of us, who would believe as a result of their message. On the night of the Last Supper he prayed for them and us. *Read John 17:6-23.*

> 6"I have revealed you to those whom you gave me out of the world. They were yours; you gave them to me and they have obeyed your word. 7Now they know that everything you have given me comes from you. 8For I gave them the words you gave me and they accepted them. They knew with certainty that I came from you, and they believed that you sent me. 9I pray for them. I am not praying for the world, but for those you have given me, for they are yours. 10All I have is yours, and all you have is mine. And glory has come to me through them. 11I will remain in the world no longer, but they are still in the world, and I am coming to you. Holy

Father, protect them by the power of your name, the name you gave me, so that they may be one as we are one. [12]While I was with them, I protected them and kept them safe by that name you gave me. None has been lost except the one doomed to destruction so that Scripture would be fulfilled.

[13]"I am coming to you now, but I say these things while I am still in the world, so that they may have the full measure of my joy within them. [14]I have given them your word and the world has hated them, for they are not of the world any more than I am of the world. [15]My prayer is not that you take them out of the world but that you protect them from the evil one. [16]They are not of the world, even as I am not of it. [17]Sanctify them by the truth; your word is truth. [18]As you sent me into the world, I have sent them into the world. [19]For them I sanctify myself, that they too may be truly sanctified.

[20]"My prayer is not for them alone. I pray also for those who will believe in me through their message, [21]that all of them may be one, Father, just as you are in me and I am in you. May they also be in us so that the world may believe that you have sent me. [22]I have given them the glory that you gave me, that they may be one as we are one— [23]I in them and you in me—so that they may be brought to complete unity. Then the world will know that you sent me and have loved them even as you have loved me.

1. You have heard the statement that Christians should be "in the world but not of it." List the examples of where you find that idea throughout Jesus' prayer.

2. According to Jesus' words here, how are Christians different from people of the world? (Consider not how we *should* be different, but how we *are* different in God's eyes.)

One of Paul's favorite phrases to describe a follower of Jesus is as one who is "in Christ." When we are "in Christ" we are "a new creation" (2 Corinthians 5:17). For more examples of how we are transformed when we are "in Christ," see Romans 6:11; 8:1; Galatians 3:26-28; Ephesians 1:13; Colossians 2:9-10.

3. How would you respond to a person who says that Christians should avoid the world? Explain your response.

4. Jesus prayed that while we live in the world, we will be protected (vv. 11-12, 15). What are some dangers inherent in living for Christ in this world?

The most common and the most subtle form of worldliness among Christians is probably pride. Some of the worldliest people masquerade behind their diligent abstinence from doing the things we might think of as worldly. But they are still worldly people because their basic concern is themselves—their own comfort, their own prestige, and their own material prosperity.

5. For what reasons are believers left in the world (vv. 18, 20-21)?

6. Christ sends us into the world—into foreign territory, so to speak. What encouragement can we draw from the fact that he was sent into the world ahead of us (vv. 13, 16, 18)?

7. How does our unity in Christ (vv. 20-23) help us to avoid worldliness?

Paul reminds Christ followers that "each member belongs to all the others" (Romans 12:5). This sort of belonging creates both community and accountability.

8. Which parts of Jesus' prayer are you especially glad he prayed?

 **RESPOND**

✳ Which has been the greater temptation for you: to avoid the world or to be too much like it?

✳ Think about your natural intersections with the world: work, family, organizations, neighborhood, leisure activities, and so on. How are you doing at living "in the world" but "not of it" at those various crossroads?

✳ List some of the assets Christ gives you as you witness for him.

 **PRAY**

Thank the Lord for coming into this world when he had no obligation to do so. Pray for protection and wisdom as you live as his follower in this world.

FIRST STEPS TO GOD

THE FOLLOWING IS AN OUTLINE of the Christian message that was developed for InterVarsity Christian Fellowship. It is a useful summary to keep in mind as you share your faith. You may want to keep a copy inside your Bible. You can work on learning it with a friend or a small group. Challenge each other to learn a line or a section each week and report in when you meet.

GOD

* God loves you (John 3:16).
* God is holy and just. He punishes all evil and expels it from his presence (Romans 1:18).

HUMANITY

* God, who created everything, made us for himself, to find our purpose in fellowship with him (Colossians 1:16).
* But we rebelled and turned away from God (Isaiah 53:6). The result is separation from God (Isaiah 59:2). The penalty is eternal death (Romans 6:23).

CHRIST

* God became human in the person of Jesus Christ to restore the broken fellowship (Colossians 1:19-20). Christ lived a perfect life (1 Peter 2:22).

* Christ died as a substitute for us by paying the death penalty for our rebellion (Romans 5:8). He arose (1 Corinthians 15:3-4) and is alive today to give us a new life of fellowship with God, now and forever (John 10:10).

RESPONSE

* I must *repent* for my rebellion (Matthew 4:17).

* I must *believe* Christ died to provide forgiveness and a new life of fellowship with God (John 1:12).

* I must *receive* Christ as my Savior and Lord with the intent to obey him. I do this in prayer by inviting him into my life (Revelation 3:20).

COST

* There is no cost to you; your salvation comes to you freely (Ephesians 2:8-9).

* But it comes at a high cost to God (1 Peter 1:18-19).

* Ultimately, your response is a life of discipleship (Luke 9:23-24).

LEADING A SMALL GROUP

LEADING A BIBLE DISCUSSION can be an enjoyable and rewarding experience. But it can also be intimidating—especially if you've never done it before. If this is how you feel, you're in good company.

Remember when God asked Moses to lead the Israelites out of Egypt? Moses replied, "Please send someone else" (Exodus 4:13)! But God gave Moses the help (human and divine) he needed to be a strong leader.

Leading a Bible discussion is not difficult if you follow certain guidelines. You don't need to be an expert on the Bible or a trained teacher. The suggestions listed below can help you to effectively fulfill your role as leader—and enjoy doing it.

PREPARING FOR THE STUDY

1. As you study the passage before the group meeting, ask God to help you understand it and apply it in your own life. Unless this happens, you will not be prepared to lead others. Pray too for the various members of the group. Ask God to open your hearts to the message of his Word and motivate you to action.

2. Read the introduction to the entire guide to get an overview of the subject at hand and the issues that will be explored.

3. Be ready to respond to the "Reflect" questions with a personal story or example. The group will be only as vulnerable and open as its leader.

4. Read the chapter of the companion book that is recommended at the beginning of the session.

5. Read and reread the assigned Bible passage to familiarize yourself with it. You may want to look up the passage in a Bible so that you can see its context.

6. This study guide is based on the New International Version of the Bible. It will help you and the group if you use this translation as the basis for your study and discussion.

7. Carefully work through each question in the study. Spend time in meditation and reflection as you consider how to respond.

8. Write your thoughts and responses in the space provided in the study guide. This will help you to express your understanding of the passage clearly.

9. It might help you to have a Bible dictionary handy. Use it to look up any unfamiliar words, names, or places.

10. Take the final (application) study questions and the "Respond" portion of each study seriously. Consider what this means for your life, what changes you may need to make in your lifestyle, or what actions you can take in your church or with people you know. Remember that the group will follow your lead in responding to the studies.

LEADING THE STUDY

1. Be sure everyone in your group has a study guide and a Bible. Encourage the group to prepare beforehand for each discussion by reading the introduction to the guide and by working through the questions for that session.

2. At the beginning of your first time together, explain that these studies are meant to be discussions, not lectures. Encourage the members of the group to participate. However, do not put pressure on those who may be hesitant to speak during the first few sessions.

3. Begin the study on time. Open with prayer, asking God to help the group understand and apply the passage.

4. Have a group member read aloud the introductory paragraph at the beginning of the discussion. This will remind the group of the topic of the study.

5. Discuss the "Reflect" questions before reading the Bible passage. These kinds of opening questions are important for several reasons. First, there is usually a stiffness that needs to be overcome before people will begin to talk openly. A good question will break the ice.

   Second, most people will have lots of different things going on in their minds (dinner, an exam, an important meeting coming up, how to get the car fixed) that have nothing to do with the study. A creative question will get their attention and draw them into the discussion.

   Third, opening questions can reveal where our thoughts or feelings need to be transformed by Scripture. That is why it is important not to read the passage before the "Reflect" questions are asked. The passage will tend to color the honest reactions people would otherwise give, because they feel they are supposed to think the way the Bible does.

6. Have a group member read aloud the Scripture passage.

7. As you ask the questions, keep in mind that they are designed to be used just as they are written. You may simply read them aloud. Or you may prefer to express them in your own words.

   There may be times when it is appropriate to deviate from the study guide. For example, a question may already have been answered. If so, move on to the next question. Or someone may raise an important question not covered in the guide. Take time to discuss it, but try to keep the group from going off on tangents.

8. Avoid offering the first answer to a study question. Repeat or rephrase questions if necessary until they are clearly understood. An eager group quickly becomes passive and silent if members think the leader will give all the *right* answers.

9. Don't be afraid of silence. People may need time to think about the question before formulating their answers.

10. Don't be content with just one answer. Ask, "What do the rest of you think?" or, "Anything else?" until several people have given answers to a question. You might point out one of the study sidebars to help spur discussion; for example, "Does the quotation on page twelve provide any insight as you think about this question?"

11. Acknowledge all contributions. Be affirming whenever possible. Never reject an answer. If it is clearly off-base, ask, "Which verse led you to that conclusion?" or, "What do the rest of you think?"

12. Don't expect every answer to be addressed to you, even though this will probably happen at first. As group members become more at ease, they will begin to truly interact with each other. This is one sign of healthy discussion.

13. Don't be afraid of controversy. It can be stimulating! If you don't resolve an issue completely, don't be frustrated. Move on and keep it in mind for later. A subsequent study may solve the problem.

14. Try to periodically summarize what the group has said about the passage. This helps to draw together the various ideas mentioned and gives continuity to the study. But don't preach.

15. When you come to the application questions at the end of each "Study" section, be willing to keep the discussion going by describing how you have been affected by the study. It's important that we each apply the message of the passage to ourselves in a specific way.

    Depending on the makeup of your group and the length of time you've been together, you may or may not want to discuss the "Respond" section. If not, allow the group to read it and reflect on it silently. Encourage members to make specific commitments and to write them in their study guide. Ask them the following week how they did with their commitments.

16. Conclude your time together with conversational prayer. Ask for God's help in following through on the commitments you've made.

17. End the group discussion on time.

Many more suggestions and helps are found in The Big Book on Small Groups *by Jeffrey Arnold.*

SUGGESTED RESOURCES

Jerram Barrs, *The Heart of Evangelism*

Beau Crosetto, *Beyond Awkward: When Talking About Jesus Is Outside Your Comfort Zone*

Jessica Leep Fick, *Beautiful Feet: Unleashing Women to Everyday Witness*

Will Metzger, *Tell the Truth: The Whole Gospel Wholly by Grace Communicated Truthfully and Lovingly*, 4th ed.

J. P. Moreland and Tim Muehlhoff, *The God Conversation: Using Stories and Illustrations to Explain Your Faith*, rev. and exp. ed.

Rebecca Manley Pippert, *Out of the Saltshaker and Into the World: Evangelism as a Way of Life*

Rick Richardson, *Reimagining Evangelism: Inviting Friends on a Spiritual Journey*

THE IVP SIGNATURE COLLECTION

Since 1947 InterVarsity Press has been publishing thoughtful Christian books that serve the university, the church, and the world. In celebration of our seventy-fifth anniversary, IVP is releasing special editions of select iconic and bestselling books from throughout our history.

RELEASING IN 2019

Basic Christianity (1958)
JOHN STOTT

How to Give Away Your Faith (1966)
PAUL E. LITTLE

RELEASING IN 2020

The God Who Is There (1968)
FRANCIS A. SCHAEFFER

This Morning with God (1968)
EDITED BY CAROL ADENEY AND BILL WEIMER

The Fight (1976)
JOHN WHITE

Free at Last? (1983)
CARL F. ELLIS JR.

The Dust of Death (1973)
OS GUINNESS

The Singer (1975)
CALVIN MILLER

RELEASING IN 2021

Knowing God (1973)
J. I. PACKER

Out of the Saltshaker and Into the World
(1979) REBECCA MANLEY PIPPERT

A Long Obedience in the Same Direction
(1980) EUGENE H. PETERSON

More Than Equals (1993)
SPENCER PERKINS AND CHRIS RICE

Between Heaven and Hell (1982)
PETER KREEFT

Good News About Injustice (1999)
GARY A. HAUGEN

RELEASING IN 2022

Hearing God (1999)
DALLAS WILLARD

The Challenge of Jesus (1999)
N. T. WRIGHT

The Heart of Racial Justice (2004)
BRENDA SALTER McNEIL AND
RICK RICHARDSON

Sacred Rhythms (2006)
RUTH HALEY BARTON

Habits of the Mind (2000)
JAMES W. SIRE

True Story (2008)
JAMES CHOUNG

RELEASING IN 2023

Scribbling in the Sand (2002)
MICHAEL CARD

Jesus Through Middle Eastern Eyes
(2008) KENNETH E. BAILEY

The Next Worship (2015)
SANDRA MARIA VAN OPSTAL

Delighting in the Trinity (2012)
MICHAEL REEVES

Strong and Weak (2016)
ANDY CROUCH

Liturgy of the Ordinary (2016)
TISH HARRISON WARREN

Plus a surprise volume to be selected by reader vote

IVP SIGNATURE BIBLE STUDIES

As companions to the IVP Signature Collection, IVP Signature Bible Studies feature the inductive study method, equipping individuals and groups to explore the biblical truths embedded in these books.

Basic Christianity Bible Study
JOHN STOTT

How to Give Away Your Faith Bible Study
PAUL E. LITTLE

The Singer Bible Study, CALVIN MILLER

Knowing God Bible Study, J. I. PACKER

**Out of the Saltshaker and Into the World
Bible Study,** REBECCA MANLEY PIPPERT

**A Long Obedience in the Same Direction
Bible Study,** EUGENE H. PETERSON

Good News About Injustice Bible Study
GARY A. HAUGEN

Hearing God Bible Study
DALLAS WILLARD

The Heart of Racial Justice Bible Study
BRENDA SALTER McNEIL AND
RICK RICHARDSON

True Story Bible Study, JAMES CHOUNG

The Next Worship Bible Study
SANDRA MARIA VAN OPSTAL

**Jesus Through Middle Eastern Eyes
Bible Study,** KENNETH E. BAILEY

Strong and Weak Bible Study
ANDY CROUCH